THE ABC'S OF A SMART BUDGET

The Easy Way for a Happier Life

NEZHA CHERQAOUA

2018

TO ALL THOSE STRUGGLING IN LIFE
LOOKING FOR INNER PEACE.

****

"WHEN EVERYTHING SEEMS TO BE AGAINST
YOU, REMEMBER THAT THE PLANE TAKES OFF
IN THE WIND AND NOT WITH HIM"
-HENRY FORD-

Table of Contents

DEDICATION

I am grateful:

-To the hard times that taught me valuable lessons along the way. Because of these moments I convinced myself that these difficulties are only opportunities to be stronger.

-To all my mistakes that lighten up the right path for me. I knew, that along my way, these obstacles helped me to reach my full potential, I learned that we grow when we face challenges.

-To the people who did created difficulties on my way; those who gave me stress and turned my life upside down.

Because of these people:

I understood that the straight line is the end of life, that the ups and downs are a symbol that the heart is still beating.

Because of these people; I turned these obstacles into a springboard to gain momentum and move forward every time I fall. I realized that great pains could become great strengths, that the difficulties

only add value to my life, that the challenge is none other than effort, action and perseverance.
It was through the challenge and the determination I realized that at last I was living.

NEZHA

INTRODUCTION

*"Being happy doesn't mean everything is Perfect,
and it never did. It means you've decided to look
beyond the Imperfections"*
-Unknown-

This Book is a result of my own personal experience.
During the earlier period of my life the way I manage
money was somewhat random, limited to the daily living
expenses (housing, food, clothing, transportation and
some various expenses) I was living to eat. Whenever there
is an increase in my income, there is some improvement in
These expenses but there was almost total neglect in other
expenses like hobbies, outgoings or traveling.

That period was followed by hard times which turned my
life upside down. I faced hard situations, many difficulties,
but they gave me lessons that I could not learn at school.
It was a necessary chapter in my life to understand the real

meaning of it. It was a kind of motivation that pushed me to reconsider everything, make a complete change in my life and then reorganize it in a way that I put myself in the place where I am supposed to be.

Finding my true vocation "eating to live" and taking care of myself; In a word I change my life from just "TO BE" into "WELL-BEING".

To overcome these difficulties, I started a new financial management so that I could go on, otherwise it's despair and surrender.

It's important to set goals before taking the first step to execute this budget planning, life makes sense when you have a goal moving towards it.
Implementing and following my budget consistently made me able to control my money rather than to be controlled by my money.

THE MOTIVATING POWERS

"Do not look for happiness, just find balance. The balance is an active posture between opposing forces creating harmony"

Every one's life is a constant and continuous flow between two poles: production and consumption.

Many of us associate production and consumption with the monetary factor, but there are also other factors that act either actively or passively and that have a significant impact on this production-consumption flow. It is a result of the interaction between axes that represent the active and motivating powers of the individual.

THE POWER OF THE MIND OR THOUGHTS:
It is the most important power. It reflects the individual's perceptions, actions and behaviors. It varies from one person to another, it could be positive as well as negative, constructive or destructive. It is a whole process of knowledge, thoughts, ideas, feelings and everything that depends on our mind.

THE POWER OF TIME:
It is an incessant flow power; it begins to take effect since the first breath and stops with the last one. It's the only world currency. It is unchangeable and invariable; it is twenty-four hours for anyone. This power is likely to become manipulative due to a poor management. It can

only be controlled by the mere means of good management.

THE POWER OF MONEY:
It is a circle between profit and loss. It is the strongest manipulator, it can easily become the boss, master our thoughts by controlling our behavior and thereby blocking the other powers. With a good management it is possible to control it and limit its dominance to avoid falling into the abyss of monetary alienation.

The power's management varies from one person to another according to each one personality and priorities. there are those who focus and pay full attention to only one of these powers.
It becomes the leader dominating the other powers, thus controlling the individual, his thoughts and behavior and even his ethics.
Due to carelessness or mismanagement, many people could be controlled and dominated by the power of time or the power of money, thus declining all the mental strength of the mind power.

The INNER PEACE

Each of us is looking for his own happiness but he can focus on one of these powers neglecting the others.

How to manage the relationship between these powers: The feedback relationship and the positive interconnection between these three powers help achieve balance and harmony.

The higher the degree of harmony, the greater the zone of convergence of powers, the greater the inner power of the individual and the feeling of peace and happiness.

Happiness is not an accumulation of joy, it is the inner power to spread the feeling of harmony throughout the body.

I have called the " harmony zone" the intersection of the three powers that have the greatest impact on our attitudes, our feelings, in a word on our life.

The human vocation is not limited to production and consumption, it is greater than such a simple relationship. The human vocation is managing the three opposing powers and establishing a good balance between them, to attend the inner peace. These powers could be active or passive, either they complement and reinforce each other, interact with each other creating "the zone of harmony". Expanding or to enlarge "the zone of harmony" depends on this relationship. Maintain a positive, healthy and balanced relationship between the three powers.

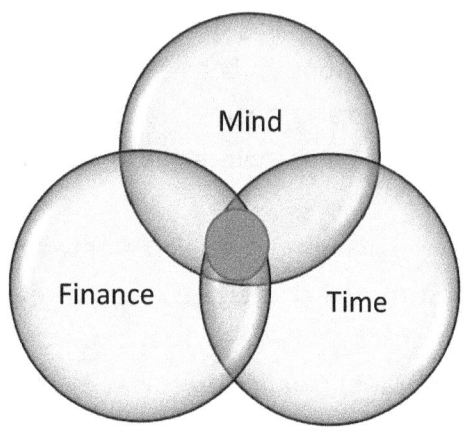

"The zone of Harmony"

The inner power is the force that results from a **healthier** mind, a healthier finance and a perfect time management. The inner power increases your health, peace and happiness.

THE UNIVERSEL QUESTION:

Does money make happiness?

"Money is a terrible master but an excellent servant"

-P. T. BURNUM-

Some chapters of our life force us to question ourselves, to take a new look at our lives and to reconsider our priorities.

Most people think that happiness is to have a lot of money. They spend most of their time thinking about how to make money, working harder to have more and be comfortable. but no matter how much we get, it never seems enough; we never felt fulfilled. We always want more money; more things; which means more stress.

Making the choice to be happy is within the reach of all of us, it does not require a lot of money or to be rich. Happiness is not to have everything we want but to love and appreciate what we have. It is not how much money we have but it is the impact of money on our lives and on the other's life.

Happiness is a state of mind, a way to grow through life. It's a nice feeling in our body after reaching the harmony that depends on the balance between certain opposing forces.
Do not look for happiness around you, it is not something readymade; it comes from your own actions.

Enjoy what you have, turn difficulties into a ladder to rise and build yourself, then the door for happiness will be opened inside of you.

Do not give up if you do so you will destroy yourself.

ALL IS ABOUT LEARNING

" Anyone who stops learning is old, whether at twenty or eighty. Anyone who keeps learning stays young. The greatest thing in life is to keep your mind young. "

–Henry Ford–

Most people make resolutions to progress and change for the better, most of us makes plans to succeed and be happy believing that happiness and success is being Rich. But most of the time there's no changes or improvements.

Success is not the plans to be made; it's a whole process that's requires a lot of effort. Currently there is many methods and programs of personal development to help those who are looking for a well-being.

Many people spend lots of money to learn how to progress and achieve their goals. They neglect the simplest way but the most powerful to do so. The way we manage our expenses has a lot more impact than most people think. Our expenses guide the meaning of our life.

> *"Do not give me a fish but teach me fishing"*
> *Chinese wisdom*

When you give something to someone you will just help him for a limited time but if you teach him skills and abilities they will be used forever.

We do not learn from anyone, we must look for the right person: the one who perform what we need to learn. We can learn from the other's experiences.

All is about learning;

You can learn anything at any time, just look for the qualified sources to learn from.

Do you want to change in depth your way of being? Do you want to progress? It is possible, and it can be learned.

This small Book is to put you on the right path, to teach you how to change your lifestyle by having a healthy and prosperous relationship with money.

How to make money at the service of your success and your happiness?

LEARN:

- Get guidelines and tips (you will find many guidelines and tips in this eBook)
- Be assisted by someone competent.

PRACTICE:

- Make and try different budget plans.
- Execute and practice your plans.

PERFORM:

- Control your spending.
- Enjoy your life
- Improve yourself.

THE BIG STEP FOR SELF-IMPROVEMENT

"Happiness is not in the mere possession of money; it lies in the joy of achievement, in the thrill of creative effort"

-Franklin D. ROOSVELT-

W e are undergoing changes despite ourselves, we must take steps to freely choose to evolve in the direction that we deem desirable.

The changes could be made by:

- Modifying certain behaviors and thoughts.
- Set a meaningful goal to motivate your efforts, with the promise of a fair reward for these efforts.

Three keys are primordial for the big step to self-improvement witch lead to success and make your life happier.

TURN ON YOUR BRAIN

"Anxiety does not stop the pain of tomorrow, but it definitely steals today's pleasure"   *-Dale CARNEGIE-*

The thought is your own perception of a specific action, and the behavior is the way you bring that perception into reality.
Never neglect the power of your thoughts.

- Say **"YES"** to positive thoughts: they will give you greater energy and more initiative.
- Training your brain make it malleable and solid.
- Insert in your brain the best values and the best believes.
- Learn new and better-adapted behaviors.
- Free your mind from anxiety.
- Keep the stress away from your life and Start your money budget to meet your financial goals.

MANAGE AND ORGANIZE YOUR TIME

"if you don't make the time to work in creating the life you want, you are eventually going to be forced to spend a LOT of time dealing with a life you don't want"
-Kevin NGO-

- There is always enough time when it is well used.
- You can make more money, but you can't make more time.
- Time is the only currency of your life: you are the only one who can determine how it can be spent.
- Invest your time in the right things.

MANAGE YOUR MONEY

"those who don't manage their money will always work for those who do"   *-Dave RAMSEY-*

The way you manage your money is the most important thing in your long-term investment success.

- Plan your budget.
- Make a list of your priorities.
- Think before spending.
- Control your spending.
- Save and Invest

THE SMART BUDGET

"Not everything that can be counted counts, and not everything that counts can be counted"

-Albert EINSTEIN-

T he "ABC's of a smart budget" is a structured and logical financial management. It fills the brain with positive thoughts and optimism.

The ABC's of a smart budget would:
- Give you more control on money management, on your thoughts and your time management.
- Help you planning and managing Priorities.
- Managing time effectively and organizing activities that can help increase productivity and achieve goals. It is important that you strive to acquire the basic time management skills and develop your abilities to achieve the highest number of goals in the shortest time possible.
- The continuity and the perseverance would make a positive impact on the way you think as well as on your well-being. However small or simple the changes will become bigger.
- Lead your life in the right direction: as you start achieving your goals and increasing your positive thoughts, your

brain grows stronger and becomes able to make the right decisions.

Never underestimate the power of your mind, it could change your life for the best by stepping on the path of success and happiness.

The EASY WAY for MONEY MANAGEMENT

> *"Three grand essentials to happiness in this life are: something to do, something to love, and something to hope for"*
> *-Joseph ADDISON-*

The monitoring of a well-maintained budget is necessary to have good results:

- Expenses control.
- Balanced budget.
- Less gap between the forecast expenses and expenses realized which leads to savings.

If all your money goes into leisure spending, you will struggle when it comes to ensure the essential expenses and to save.

The "ABC's of a smart budget" is the balance between three actions:

I spend - I enjoy - I plan

It needs just a little work: three necessary lists help you to meet your financial goals.

- A- What I need
- B- What I want
- C- What I plan.

Set up three goals:

- A- Change your life by controlling your expenses.
- B- Improve your lifestyle.
- C- Progress through life

THREE LISTS: THREE STEPS A – B – C

*"There are two ways to be comfortable:
raising one's income to one's desires or
lowering one's desires to one's income."*

–Jules FIAUX–

No matter how much money we make, it never seems to be enough. Managing your money start with making different lists.

Making a list help you to track your spending: it shows you where your money goes.

1- Write down all your income and calculate the monthly average. It might be the salary, the social allocations or any other source of income.
2- On another paper, put down all your expenses on a time basis: the monthly, the annual or occasional ones.

   - The monthly expenses:
Most of our daily and weekly expenses will be calculated by month. the amount of some are stable (housing, car payment....)

The amount of some others may vary (food, utilities, bills, gas...)

-The annual expenses:
Anything that we pay once or twice a year (insurance, registration, taxes...)

-The occasional expenses:
These are the expenses that we do any time or by occasion (clothing and accessories, hobbies, outings, traveling, extra and various expenses...)

The LIST OF EXPANDITURE/ On time basis

Expense	Monthly	Annually	Occas-ionally	Other
Rent	*			
Electricity	*			
Water	*			
Gas	*			
Internet	*			
Groceries	*			
Food & drinks	*			
Phone	*			
Cable TV	*			
Car payment	*			
Gas	*			
Insurance		*		
Registration		*		
Maintenance			*	
Public transportation	*			
School	*			
Books			*	
Courses	*			

The LIST OF ALL EXPENSES (continued)

Expense	Monthly	Annually	Occas-ionally	Other
Health insurance		*		
medication				*
Supplement				*
Massages			*	
Fitness	*			
Sport	*			
Beauty supplies			*	
Restaurant			*	
Movies			*	
Games			*	
Travelling			*	
Any membership		*		
Gifts			*	
Any other expenses				*
cloths			*	
Accessories			*	

Add or remove from the list above as needed.

3- Make different categories from the list above.

CATEGORY	EXPENSES
HOUSING	Rent or mortgage – utilities (electricity – gas – water.)
FOOD	Food – groceries - drinks
TRANSPORTATION	Car payment - gas – insurance –registration - maintenance Or public transportation (bus-metro-train.)
BILLS	Phone – internet – cable TV...
CLOTHING	Cloths and accessories
EDUCATION	School – courses – books – electronics...
HEALTH CARE	Health insurance – medication - supplement
SELFCARE	Sport – fitness – Spa – beauty supplies
DIVERTISSEMENT	Hobbies – games – club membership
OUTINGS	Restaurant – movies
TRAVELLING	
DONATION	Donation - gifts
EXTRAS	Various/unexpected expenses

4- LIST YOUR PRIORITIES

To meet the balance in your budget you need to respect the priorities. Start your final list with the most important expenses.

PRIORITY #1: The DAILY LIVING EXPENSES

They are the expenses that are a must, they make our daily living; From housing and utilities to the food and drinks.

PRIORITY #2: the NECESSARY EXPENSES

All the expenses that can make our daily life easier and more comfortable. Transportation, the bills (phone – Wi-fi and TV cable), clothing, accessories and health care.

PRIORITY #3: SELFCARE / PERSONNAL EXPENSES

Are the expenses to keep you healthy and in good shape: beauty care, sport and fitness.

PRIORITY #4: DIVERTISSEMENT and LEISURE:

They are the expenses that bring joy in your life and help you gain intellectual and cultural wealth; as outings, hobbies, games and travelling.

PRIORITY #5: EXTRAS and VARIOUS EXPENSES

The other various expenses that are not expected.

5- Assign a percentage for each category of expenses:

How much money you will spend for each expense?

6- The final list is the set of all the priorities that will be achieved over three steps:

Step "A"
What I need and what is necessary for my daily living: means the essential expenses for the daily living like food, housing, transportation, clothing...etc.

Step "B"
What I want or what I love to do: the expenses that depend of my choice. Their impact will be positive, bringing joy in my life. But if I choose not to do these expenses it doesn't harm my living in any way.

Step "C"
What I plan and what I hope for:
Planning the expenses for a better future helps improving your lifestyle.
To make plans; you need to:
- Set goals.
- To achieve your goals, you need to save money.
- To save money; you need to manage your money by putting a budget.

"The ABC's of a smart budget" is the perfect way to manage money, for everyone and for whatever income. It is a good way for the beginner to become an expert in the money management.

> *"an expert in any thing was once a beginner"*
> *Helen HAYAS*

STEP "A" SPENDING

"Something to do"

"The highest use of capital is not to make money, but to make money do more for the betterment of life."

–Henri Ford–

T

o spend money, we need to work and make money.

What you need comes first, what you want will be the next.

We always want more, and we never felt fulfilled, we would never be happy because happiness is not to have what we want but it's about loving what we have.

To spend the money wisely; do not go over your budget: calculate how much you have, how much you need and how much you can save.

Calculate spending activates your left brain and logical thinking which means more control over your expenses and more control over your money management.

The Step "A" relates to the expenses on the first list "A". It is only about what you need and what is necessary.

The other things you want, and you love to do may get you over the spending budget, put them down on the list "B" or "C".

CHANGE YOUR LIFE BY CONTROLLING YOUR EXPENSES

LIVING EXPENSES: the priority #1

The expenses that are a must, they make our daily living.

PRIORITY #1	CATEGORY	EXPENSE
DAILY LIVING EXPENSES	HOUSING	Rent
		Mortgage
	UTILITIES	Electricity
		Gas
		Water
	FOOD	All groceries, food and drinks

THE NECESSARY EXPENSES: the priority #2

All the expenses that can make our daily life easier and more comfortable.

PRIORITY #2	CATEGORY	EXPENSE
NECESSARY EXPENSES	TRANSPORTATION	Car payment
		Gas
		Insurance
		Registration/ maintenance
		Bus – taxi – train...
	BILLS	Phone
		Internet
		TV cable...
	CLOTHING	Clothes
		accessories
	HEALTH CARE	Health insurance
		Medication
		supplement

HOW MUCH YOU NEED?
LIST "A"

You are rich when you are happy and content with what you have.

If the step "A" took all your income, you will spend all your time working to get money and spend it on just your living expenses. You will remain among the category of people who are "LIVING to EAT". The people who are only caring about how much food they can get.

(Percentage of expenses / income)

LIST "A"	CATEGORY	EXPENSE	%
DAILY LIVING EXPENSES 45%	HOUSING	Rent	28%
		mortgage	
	UTILITIES	Electricity	02%
		Gas	
		Water	
	FOOD	Groceries	15%
		food	
		drinks	
NECESSARY EXPENSES 18%	TRANSPORTATION	Car payment	12%
		Gas	
		Insurance	
		Registration/ maintenance	
	BILLS	Phone	02%
		Internet	
		TV cable…	
	CLOTHING	Clothes	02%
		accessories	
	HEALTH CARE	Health insurance	02%
		Medication / supplement	

SPENDING

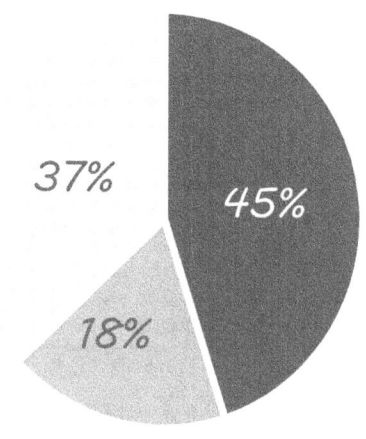

LIST "A" percentage

37%   45%

18%

· LIVING EXPENSES   · NECESSARY EXPENSES   INCOME LEFT

SPENDING TIPS

1- Tracking your spending: it shows you where your money goes and allows you to find opportunities to cut back.

2- Truck bills: by avoiding delays you can avoid extra charges and fees.

3- Renting is an expense but buying a house is an investment. Look for the rent that you can afford, never exceed the amount designed for it. Pay less for the rent but you can pay more for the mortgage: you can allow yourself an extra margin over the percentage designed for housing.

4- Avoid "junk food": it is more money and more health problems.

5- Promoting a healthy diet and good food means less spending on the category "healthcare" by decreasing your needs to doctors and medication.

6- Clothing: Buy only what is necessary, don't go over the budget for the category clothing and accessories.

7- Simplify your needs: the unnecessary expenses are a waste of money.

8- If your income is small and you need a car you can buy a used one but good enough to do the job. If you want a nice new car, do not forget to put it on your third list (**C**).

9- Reduce your purchases: lower your expenses by putting your desires on the list "**B**" or list "**C**".

10- Plan for the big purchases and list them by priorities.

STEP "B": ENJOYING

"What I love"

"enjoy the littles things in life, because one day you will look back and realize they were the big things"

-Kurt VONNEGUT-

SPENDING WHILE ATTRACTING JOY

> *"It's not in doing what you like, but in liking what you do that is the secret of happiness."*

T urn toward the beautiful side of your life; live the moment without dwelling on the negative things but rather strengthen the positive ones.

The step "B" makes you more productive and efficient by having an Impact on time management. Knowing how to control money and expenses predisposes us to control our time and spend it positively while being active.

Control your time by:

- Make the best use of your time between work and pleasure: have enough time to do what brings joy in your life.

- Give more value to your time by loving what you do and living your day in the fullest.

- Taking care of yourself by giving more time to your selfcare (sports - exercise- spa)
- Enjoying good and healthy food.
- Sharing good moments with your family and loved ones.
- Making memories: a sweet memory has always been   a happiness.
- Experience, enjoy and discover by traveling and visiting other places.
- Making your time suitable to gain intellectual and cultural wealth.

How much you usually enjoy

By fulfilling the step B (what I love), you will be among the category of people who "Eat to LIVE". The ones who care about how much they enjoy and how happy the home is? Giving time to yourself promote your physical, mental and emotional life.

IMPROVE YOUR LIFESTYLE

SELFCARE: priority #3:
Sport, fitness, beauty care, spa and care supplies are the most expenses that goes in the selfcare category.

DISTRACTION and LEISURE: priority #4

Enjoy your hobbies and outings. Enjoy your time with your family and friends (restaurants, movies, games....)

EXTRAS and OTHER EXPENSES: priority #5:

All the other and unexpected expenses are to be listed in this category.

Percentage of expenses / income.

PRIORITY	CATEGORY	EXPENSE	%
#3	SELFCARE	Sport - fitness Beauty care...	05%
#4	LEISURE and DISTRACTION	Hobbies- outings Movies- games	05%
#5	EXTRAS and other expenses	Fees - services unexpected expenses.	02%

LIST "B"

LIST "B" percentage

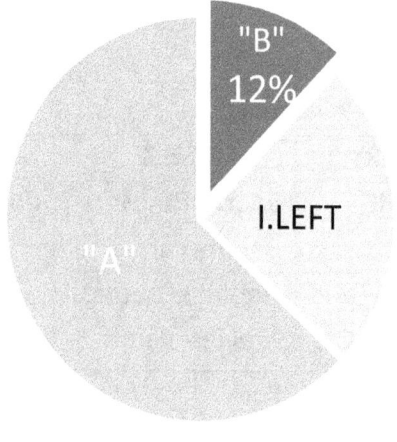

"B"
12%

I.LEFT

- "B" ENJOYING
  INCOME LEFT
- "A" spending

TIPS FOR SPENDING WHILE ENJOYING

1- Respect the budget allowed to the enjoying expenses.
2- Do not go over the percentage for list "B".
3- Schedule your entertainment.
4- Plan your outings and activities.
5- Make a list of places you love to visit all year long.
6- Promote free leisure and outings (picnics, barbecue at the parc…)
7- Promote free activities and sports (walking, biking, hiking…)
8- Get the annual pass for places that you can visit any time along the year.
9- Look for free or low-cost programs that you may qualify for.
10- Go to the library.

STEP "C": PLANNING AND IMPROVING

"Something to hope for"

"happiness is not in the mere possession of money, it lies in the joy of achievement, in the thrill of creative effort"

–Franklin D. ROOSVELT–

C ultivate your happiness by mastering the three lists or steps A B C.

The step "C" is made from:
- The 25% left from your income; you must save before spending.
- All the money left from your expenses "A" & "B" goes to the saving part.
- Make more opportunities to save more money with changing some bad habits.

 Planning a good future for you and your family to improve your life is your choice: take positive attitudes and make the right decisions.

To improve you need to save and invest.

By Saving and investing you will raise the curve of your revenue and have a positive impact on the future.

Saving money educate your behavior looking for the way how you will be happy, caring about how happy you are makes you a financial expert.

The BIG STEP to MAKE A CHANGE:

> *"the habit of saving is itself an education. It fosters every virtue, teaches self-denial, cultivates the sense of order, trains to forethought and so broadens the mind"*
> *Thornton T. Munger*

SAVE

To change your habits and your life, you need to save.

Saving starts with setting goals:
To save money you need to put specific goals. You should believe that your goals are achievable. Always move towards your goals, do not give up, do not despair. When you believe this, your mind will find ways to help you achieve these goals.

The decision you take to save money will affect your financial future; you will see how the savings will motivate you to save more money.

1-   Short-term savings:

Planning to improve; starts with the short-term savings.
It is the amount of money saved on a short time (from three months to one year) to invest in short goals and small projects.

2-   Long term savings:

The money you save for a long-term allows the large amount expenses. It will be for large amounts and big projects:
The long-term savings will make a big change in your life. Set up your goals for three years, five years, ten years and more.

INVEST

How happy you will be?
Progress through life by improving yourself and getting a better position. If you have a career that you fit in it means less stress and less pressure.

SHORT-TERM INVESTEMENT

PERSONAL DEVELOPMENT:

- Enroll in advanced program studies and performance courses
- Learn new skills that allow you to earn more money and be more independent.

RELAXING:

- Travelling: to relax and recharge your batteries.

- Save money for holidays deals and go on a trip.

BIG EXPENSES:

- Make a list of all the big purchases for the year and prioritize what you need.
- Save money for big projects.

LONG-TERM INVESTMENT

The long-term savings will be for the big investment:

Large amount projects:

- The purchase of a house.
- The purchase of a new car.
- The purchase of furniture.

Creating another source of income:

- Invest in your own business.

SAY "NO" TO THE BAD HABITS

Bad habits **DESTROY** your **HEALTH**
and **DESTROY** your **POCKET**

Changing bad habits means creating health in your life and money in the jar.

A bad habit is a desire that – in the long run – turns into a need that we cannot do without.

If you are used to get a drink at the gas station or in a coffee shop, to get the junk food or smoking at any time of the day; you need to take a moment to realize how much you are spending. Putting limits on it by putting that money in the glove box of your car or in a jar (after you come home) helps you to save. Modest sums that are regularly saved and invested quickly produce a small jackpot.

It requires some training to get used to it.

If you are used to spend $3 a day, it will be more than $90 per month and more than $1000 per year.

Spending $5 a day will be 150 per month and more than 1800 per year.

This amount will be pretty good to pay your insurance or registration car, or to get something that you have dreamed of.

CHANGE bad habits in GOOD ones
CONTROL yourself………Get MOTIVATED

1- CHANGE BAD HABITS:

The bad habits provide joy, getting used to this joy gives you a sense of satisfaction. You must know that it is a temporary and superficial pleasure. It silences this need for a short and limited time.

To get rid of bad habits, you need to find alternatives. You may develop a sense of what brings true happiness and find more satisfaction in saving than in spending.

Stopping bad habits could be a money saving, replace them with the good ones TURN IN enjoying.

2- CONTROL YOURSELF:

Saving that money would help you to control yourself. The need of that pleasure would be fulfilled in a positive way by following the next step.

3- REWARD YOURSELF and GET MOTIVATED:

Use the saved money to buy yourself something you love or give yourself a gift by buying something you dreamed for.

Start small savings for a short time, use this savings to buy a gift for yourself. Then start saving for a longer time to afford a nicer gift.

Getting yourself a massage session will gives you a good feeling of relaxation. The idea of offering yourself something may seem rewarding.

You will gain more satisfaction, more optimism and more self-confidence.

THE BIG STEP TO MAKE A DIFFERENCE

DONATION

"We make a LIVING with what we GET but we make a LIFE by what we GIVE"
- Winston CHURCHIL-

D onation is the money You give to the people in difficulty or to associations. Giving is the continuity of humanity.

to give is the exit from one's Ego toward the love of others.
Giving means more control over your money.
The amount to donate will be a **3%** of your income.
It's a small thing that you can give but it means everything in someone's else's life.

Some of us think that happiness is an accumulation of pleasures, while happiness is a feeling of joy diffused throughout the body. Accumulating pleasures concern the person "itself"; it's a limited joy by certain conditions.
But sharing pleasure with "OTHERS" is without limits or conditions.
To **GIVE** is to **SHARE** pleasure and joy, to put a smile on the other's face. It will open your inner door on your own deepest good and provide a feeling of well-being and happiness.

> *"Not all of us can do great things but we can do small things with great love"*
> *Mother TERESA*

"It's not how much you give but how much love you put into giving."

When you donate with love you make the other person happy then you get a few more happiness by the rule of attraction "what goes around comes around".

The donation makes a positive difference in the other's life as more satisfaction and happiness in yours. There is a relation between giving and happiness, the more you give, the more you share a positive energy that interact with your surrounding environment.

If you do not know how to acquire your own happiness, try to make the happiness of others. it is in the act of giving where the happiness resides.

A Chinese wisdom says:

> *" Some fragrance always lingers in the hand that gives roses"*

Just try it and you will see the difference on a long term.

SAVING TIPS

1- Save before spending.

2- Start saving from a small amount; if we do not learn to save from the little, we cannot save from much.

3- Start saving regularly as soon as possible: making saving a habit since you are young would help you continue, and you would be able to provide your own family's needs.

4- Teach your kids how to save from their pocket money.

5- Make extra savings when you get rid of contracts that you don't need (like cable TV).

6- Reduce the waste and unnecessary expenses, it is a lost money, cancel the unused memberships or subscriptions that you are not using any more.

7- Get out of debt by limiting credit cards: keep just one. If you can't control yourself, it is better to pay things in cash.

8- Take some time to reflect on things you do not necessarily need.

BUDGET EXAMPLES FOR DIFFERENT INCOMES

EXAMPLE#1:

MONTHLY INCOME: $3.000

LIST	CATEGORY EXPENSE	%	MONTHLY AMOUNT $$
A	HOUSING & utilities	30%	900
	FOOD & DRINKS	15%	450
	TRANSPORTATION	12%	360
	BILLS	02%	60
	CLOTHING/ ACCESSORIES	02%	60
	HEALTHCARE	02%	60
"A"	TOTAL	63%	1.890

LIST "A"

- Daily living expenses = ...$1.350
- Necessary expenses = ... $ 540

NB: If there is some money left after expenses on list "A" add it to the income left.

Monthly income = $3.000: list "B"

LIST "B"	CATEGORY EXPENSE	%	MONTHLY AMOUNT $$
#3	SELFCARE	05%	$150
#4	LEISURE and DISTRACTION	05%	$150
	EXTRAS EXPENSES	02%	$ 60
"B"	**TOTAL**	**12%**	**$360**

LIST "B": $ 360

- Selfcare expenses = ... **$150**
- Leisure and distraction expenses = ...**$150**
- Extras expenses: .... **$ 60**

NB: If there is some money left after expenses on list "B" add it to the income left (to use on list "C")

Monthly income = $3.000: list "C"

LIST "C"	CATEGORY	%	MONTHLY AMOUNT $$
	savings	22%	$660
	Donation & gifts	03%	$ 90
C		**25%**	**$ 750**

List "C":

Savings amount: ………………………………………. **$660**

Donation and gifts: ………………………………. **$90**

EXAMPLE #1
3 lists A-B-C

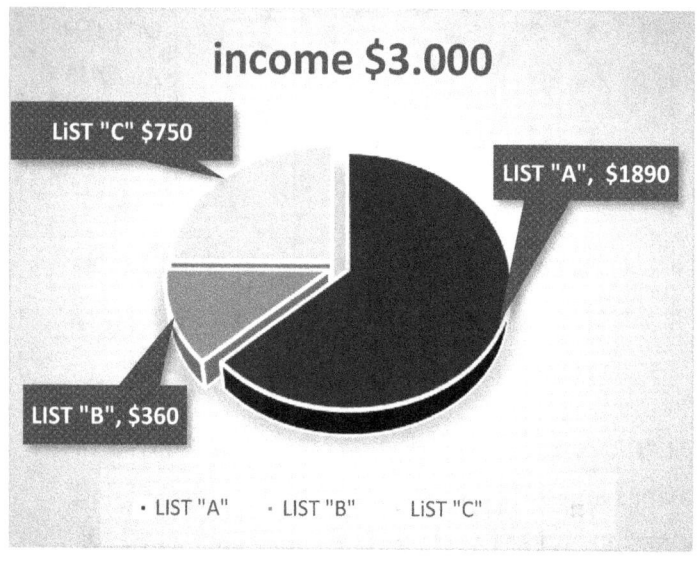

List "A" = ... **$1.890**
List "B" =.. **$ 360**
List "C" =.. **$ 750**

The EXPENSES REPARTITION
Monthly income: $3.000

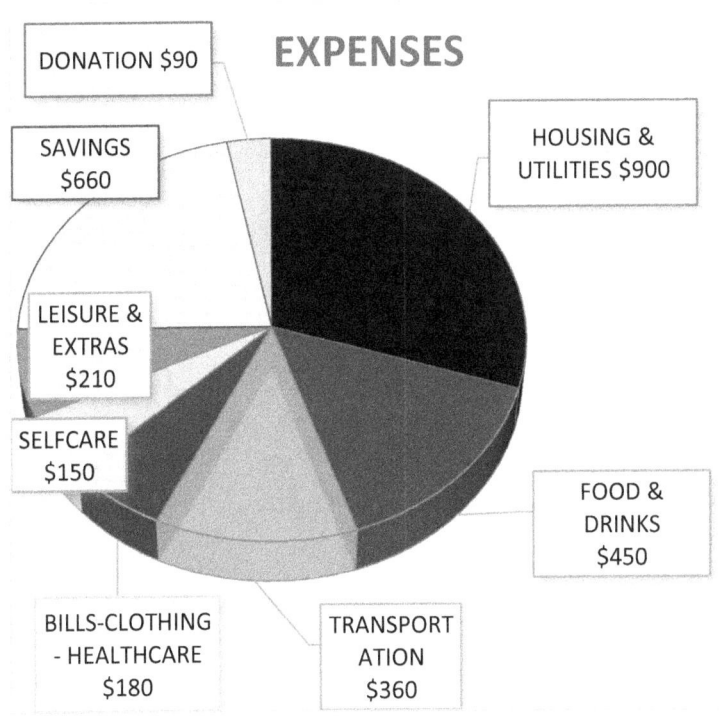

EXPENSES

DONATION $90

SAVINGS $660

HOUSING & UTILITIES $900

LEISURE & EXTRAS $210

SELFCARE $150

FOOD & DRINKS $450

BILLS-CLOTHING - HEALTHCARE $180

TRANSPORTATION $360

Housing + utilities: $900

Food + drinks: $450

Transportation: $180

Bills+ clothing+ healthcare: $180

Selfcare: $150

Leisure + extras: $120

Savings: 660

Donation + gifts: $90

MONTHLY INCOME: $5.000

LIST	CATEGORY EXPENSE	%	MONTHLY AMOUNT $$
A	HOUSING & utilities	30%	1.500
	FOOD & DRINKS	15%	750
	TRANSPORTATION	12%	600
	BILLS	02%	100
	CLOTHING / ACCESSORIES	02%	100
	HEALTHCARE	02%	100
"A"	**TOTAL**	**63%**	**3.150**

LIST "A"

- Total daily living expenses = ... **$2.250**
- Total necessary expenses =..................... **$ 900**

NB: If there is some money left after expenses on list A, add it to the income left.

MONTHLY INCOME: $5.000 = list "B"

LIST "B"	CATEGORY EXPENSE	%	MONTHLY AMOUNT $$
#3	SELFCARE	05%	$250
#4	LEISURE and DISTRACTION	05%	$250
	EXTRAS EXPENSES	02%	$100
"B"	TOTAL	12%	$ 600

LIST "B": $ $600

- Selfcare expenses =…………………………… **$250**
- Leisure and distraction expenses = ………. **$250**
- Extras expenses: ……………………………. **$100**

NB: the income left to use on list **"C"**.

BUDGET EXAMPLE: list "C"
Monthly income = $5.000:

LIST "C"	CATEGORY	%	MONTHLY AMOUNT $$
	Savings	22%	$1.100
	Donation	03%	$ 150
C		**25%**	**$ 1.250**

List "C": **$1.250**

Savings: ……………………………… ….. **$1.100**

Donation: ……………………………………. **$150**

LIST A-B-C

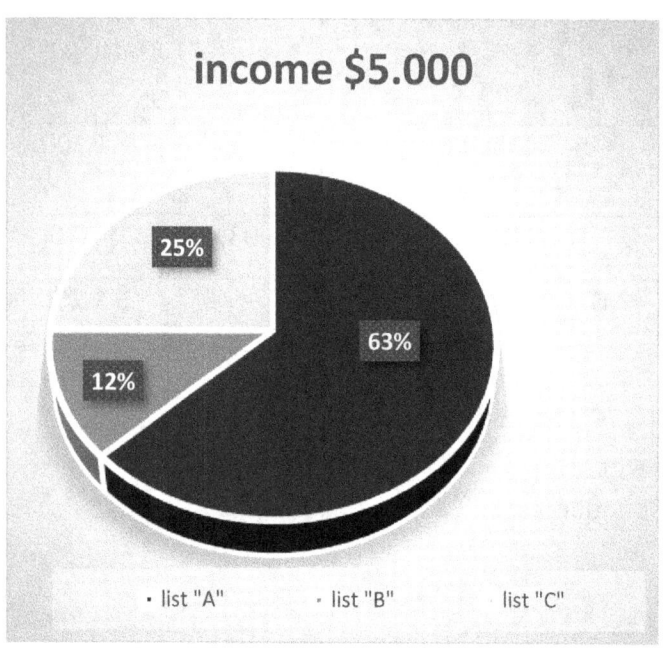

List "A" = ... **$3.150**
List "B" = ... **$ 600**
List "C" = ... **$1.250**

The EXPENSES REPARTITION:
Example #2: Income: $5.000

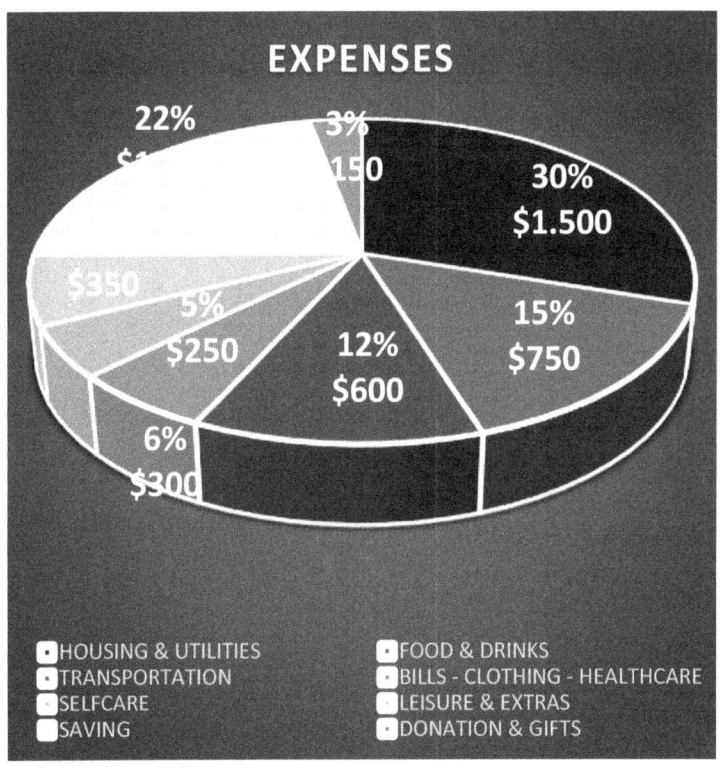

Housing + utilities: **$1.500**

Food + drinks: **$750**

Transportation: **$600**

Bills+ clothing+ healthcare: **$300**

Selfcare: **$250**

Leisure + extras: **$350**

Savings: **$1.100**

Donation + gifts: **$150**

CONCLUSION

«Your life does not get better by chance,
it's gets better by change."

-Jim ROHN-

P rogress is impossible without change. Everything we do starts with ourselves, whether it's our thoughts, our attitudes or our actions. We are in control.

Take your time to think about each action, calculate, manage and improve your finances.
Money is one of the biggest stress makers. The higher is the income, the higher are the demands and the higher is the stress.

"The ABC's of a smart budget" is a tool in the process to lower this stress, while elevating the way of thinking and changing our attitudes into a simple and positive lifestyle.
Looking forward for a better life and working hard to raise your income and improve your financial situation means that the budget must meet the needs first not the demands. You must be aware that the needs go in parallel with your financial possibilities.
If your income goes up on the quantitative line, make sure your life goes up on the qualitative line.

The budget monitoring is necessary:
After starting "the smart budget", the follow-up about three months is necessary for the budget smooth running.

Make the point, review the three lists for the step's "A" – "B" and "C".

- Inventory your expenses from the most important to the least important.
- Review the extent to which the amount allocated for these expenses has been respected.
- Achieve a lesser difference between the expected and the realized amount for any expense.

Review the proceeds of savings:

- Inventory of short and long-terms savings.
- Inventory of achievements (both short and long terms).

Adjust the budget according to the results obtained.
If the budget results are negative, set up a new one which will be more adequate.

After the first years of the smart budget's follow-up, your level of self-confidence increases, as well as your skills and your potential.

BE THE BOSS

"Money is only a tool; it will take you wherever you wish but it will not replace you as a driver"

–Ayaan RAND–

It's not about how much money you make it's about how you plan your budget and how you spend your money.

The financial problems give you more stress and make your life harder.
Since you start a good money management and start saving, you will have more control over your expenses and your money. Being in control of your money is the big stress reliever.

Be the **BOSS** and use your money as a tool not as a destination.
Yes, money could take you in better places as well as bad places; **YOU** choose your destination.

Design your life from common and small things and live your day to the fullest. Always remember that life is like a piece of cake, everyone has the ingredients but each one has his OWN and UNIQUE Way to mix them.
The way you mix these ingredients is **YOUR CHOICE**.

The LIST OF EXPANDITURE

Check up all your expenses and make your own list

Expense	Monthly	Annually	Occas-ionally	Other
Rent/mortgage				
Electricity				
Water				
Gas				
Internet				
Groceries				
Food & drinks				
Phone				
Cable TV				
Car payment				
Gas				
Insurance				
Registration				
Maintenance				
Public transportation				
School				
Books				
Courses				

The LIST OF ALL EXPENSES (continued)

Expense	Monthly	Annually	Occas-ionally	Other
Health insurance				
medication				
Supplement				
Massages				
Fitness				
Sport				
Beauty supplies				
Restaurant				
Movies				
Games				
Travelling				
Any membership				
Gifts				
Any other expenses				
cloths				
Accessories				

Set up your own priority's lists.

CATEGORY	CHECK PRIORITY				
	#1	#2	#3	#4	#5
HOUSING					
FOOD					
TRANSPORTATION					
BILLS					
CLOTHING					
EDUCATION					
HEALTH CARE					
SELFCARE					
DIVERTISSEMENT					
OUTINGS					
TRAVELLING					
DONATION					
EXTRAS					

www.ingramcontent.com/pod-product-compliance
Lightning Source LLC
Chambersburg PA
CBHW071208220526
45468CB00002B/546